PRESENTATION

To **Kristine Lochte**

From **The Glen Lochte's**

Date **April 7, 1974**

WORLD INSPIRATIONAL BOOKS

AN ORIGINAL

edited by David A. MacLennan

THE
POWER
OF
WORSHIP

by Melvin E. Wheatley, Jr.

THE WORLD PUBLISHING COMPANY

New York and Cleveland

Published by The World Publishing Company

Published simultaneously in Canada
by Nelson, Foster & Scott Ltd.

FIRST PRINTING—1970

PRINTED IN THE UNITED STATES OF AMERICA

WORLD PUBLISHING
TIMES MIRROR
NEW YORK AND CLEVELAND

ACKNOWLEDGMENTS

Scripture passages reprinted in this book are from the REVISED
STANDARD VERSION BIBLE, *copyright 1946 and 1952 by the*
Division of Christian Education of the National Council of the
Churches of Christ in the U.S.A.

CONTENTS

Introduction

Foreword

One

NOURISHING OUR SENSE OF THE SACRED

15

Two

BEING TOUGH-MINDED AND WHOLE-HEARTED

24

Three

GETTING OUR IMAGINATIONS TURNED ON

34

Four

ENCOUNTERING GOD AS A FOUR-LETTER WORD

44

Five

DOING OUR THING

54

INTRODUCTION

About the Book

MELVIN ERNEST WHEATLEY, JR., has taken for his text the comprehensive and arresting description of what it means to worship given by the late William Temple, Archbishop of Canterbury. Dr. Temple, one of this century's eminent philosophers and theologians, is reported to have made an unexpected answer to a question asked him during a conference in Washington, D.C., on his last visit to the United States. He was asked what he considered to be the Church's chief task: What was it here in the world to do above all else? In essence, this world-renowned churchman answered that in one sense the Church was not here to *do* anything; it was placed here by its divine Founder and Head to *be* something—the redeemed and redemptive company of Christ's people offering God the purest and worthiest worship of which it was capable. All else was derivative and secondary. It is also the implied conviction of Dr. Wheatley as this searching study of the rationale of worship makes clear. As his biographical sketch indicates, our author is no "otherwordly" guru or teacher of esoteric doctrine. His own record shows how deeply committed he is to furthering mental and physical health, sound education, just and fraternal racial relationships, and involvement in other social concerns.

Another distinguished preacher of the Christian gospel, the late Harry Emerson Fosdick, liked to tell theological students that he preferred the kind of preaching that is "animated conversation." In this study of dynamic worship, Melvin Wheatley engages in animated conversation with the reader. What he has written and the way in which he has written it compliment the reader. For in these pages you will find no oversimplified treatment of profound themes; he writes as an educated man aware of the sophisticated approach to religion, able to meet the sophisticate and the doubter of every degree of culture on his own ground.

His English style is clear, concise, and memorable. Consider these excerpts from his discussion: "How easy it is, because of the pressure upon us, to become so busy manipulating the world that we neglect to wonder at the world . . ." Think not only of the diction but of the truth expressed in such a statement as this: "We can open our hearts to God's love—not by arguing our heads off; but by sticking our necks out in the life of love, and by holding our hands out with love to life." Again: "Use your heads to find the truth; but use your hearts to serve the best you have been able to discover." This book's author provides guidance for the man or woman of this turbulent, often confusing society to select the food of truth in what he describes as "the cafeteria of conflicting ideologies."

Read this book carefully. Then read it again. You will have new appreciation of the centrality of the worship of God and your conviction will be deepened that "The central message of the Gospel is that God is for us." One consequence will be, to quote Dr.

Wheatley's words again, that you will realize that "For all of us— NOW is always the time for serving God, as near as the closest need and as ready as a friendly smile."

About the Author

MELVIN E. WHEATLEY, JR., is associated with the State of California and since 1942 has made it his home and the scene of his successful pastorates. Son and grandson of Methodist ministers, he has added to the excellent environment such a heritage provides an unusually creative native ability. He, as well as his many friends, would add that a strong factor in his success as pastor, preacher, civic leader, teacher, husband, and father has been the personality and support of his gifted wife Lucile. Dr. and Mrs. Wheatley have three sons, the oldest already an ordained Methodist minister.

Born in Lewisville, Pennsylvania, Dr. Wheatley received his academic education at Middletown (Delaware) High School and American University, Washington, D.C., from which he graduated A.B. *magna cum laude* in 1936. Three years later he received his bachelor of divinity degree *summa cum laude* from Drew University, Madison, N.J. He was among the first Protestant clergymen to take clinical training. His pastorates include Lincoln, Delaware; associate minister, First Methodist Church, Fresno, Centenary Methodist Church, Modesto, and Central Methodist Church, Stockton, California, and since 1954 senior minister of Westwood United Methodist Church, Los Angeles. In this beautiful cathedral-like edifice great congregations have beeen led week by week in the public worship of God and have received the Word in relevant, contemporary expression from this eloquent, thoughtful servant of Christ.

Dr. Wheatley is an effective teacher and has served as instructor and lecturer in universities and theological seminaries. As an author, he has had articles appear in important periodicals. He has written for the *Journal of Health, Physical Education* magazine, and *Recreation*. He has published the refreshing and stimulating book *Going His Way* (Fleming H. Revell Company, 1957) and a limited edition of *Our Man and the Church*. He is no ivory tower theologian; his hobbies include sports and music.

The University of the Pacific (Stockton) and American University have acknowledged his outstanding contributions in many fields by awarding him honorary doctorates. He was chosen "Clergyman of the Year" in 1958 for work done with the Mental Health Clinic. He has traveled widely, frequently as conductor of study tours of European and Middle Eastern countries. He is one of the noble company of prophets and pastors every man in "holy orders" would wish to be.

DAVID A. MACLENNAN
General Editor

Foreword

A recent cartoon pictured a Roman Catholic priest bemoaning the changes that have affected his vocation as a leader in worship. He spent eleven years learning Latin and now the mass is in English. He went to Europe to master classical chorales and now some of his parishioners want folk songs to guitar accompaniment. The cartoon goes on to caricature the numerous and various changes in the formal modes of worship in our time.

But although the settings and the liturgies of institutional worship do keep changing, the dynamics of authentic worship repeat themselves across the years. More than a quarter of a century ago, Archbishop William Temple analyzed those dynamics in a summary which is still as appropriate as it is adequate. In his *The Hope of a New World*, he wrote: ". . . if you are really worshiping at all, then you are doing just what is most needed to enable you to take your part in bringing in the new world for which we hope. For to worship is:

to quicken the conscience by the holiness of God,
to feed the mind with the truth of God,
to purge the imagination by the beauty of God,
to open the heart to the love of God,
to devote the will to the purpose of God."*

We make the Archbishop's analysis our outline for the chapters which follow.

---

* William Temple, *The Hope of a New World* (New York: The Macmillan Company, 1942), p. 30.

One

NOURISHING OUR SENSE

OF THE SACRED

"I saw the Lord . . . high and lifted up."

ISAIAH 6: 1–8

A CENTRAL affirmation of religion is that the spot on which we stand is holy ground. The days of our years are a sacred trust. Our life is a serious encounter and covenant with our Creator. We have dealings with divinity. Both the estimate of our worth and the meaning of our work are measured against this assumption.

But this assumption is not readily felt as fact in our time. How easy it is, because of the pressures upon us, to become so busy manipulating the wonders of the world that we neglect to wonder at the world; to move so fast across the stage that we neglect to ponder the plot; to become so fascinated with the fluctuation of prices that we become quite indifferent to the hierarchy of values.

With all we have within us, we must resist such pressures to let life become profane. For nothing matters much for long among people who have lost the sense that some things matter most. One of the disciplines we need to be about in our time, therefore, is to "quicken our consciences with the holiness of God" and thus to nourish the sense of the sacred which is the source of so much of our sense of significance. But how are we to do it? The surest way I know is to stop and wonder about three things—the mysteries of the world around us, the mysteries of the world within us, and the relationship between the two.

I am assuming, of course, that if we do stop and wonder we will be confronted with mysteries in the world around us. We will find phenomena which are beyond us—not in the sense that they are unfamiliar to us, for oftentimes they will be the most familiar aspects of our experience, but beyond us in the sense that we can neither adequately account for nor fully comprehend them. *THE TRINITY*

Take light, for example. Light surely is one of the most familiar phenomena of our experience. Yet who of us accounts for light or fully comprehends it? Hardly a week passes without some headline like the recent one: "Telescope on Palomar Opening Up Universe—Giant Two-Hundred-Inch Instrument Observing New Areas Photographing Billions of Objects." Among other fascinating facts reported was this note: "Fantastic collisions of galaxies that occurred millions of years ago are now being photographed by the giant telescope . . . The universe is so inconceivably immense that light from these heavenly phenomena is just now reaching the earth. The most distant object photographed to date by the telescope has been a galaxy sextillion miles away—that's thirty followed by twenty-one zeroes."

Or turn from the Palomar telescope to an atomic microscope. We learn through such an instrument (so they tell me!) that in our next breath, we shall inhale more than a thousand million, million, million atoms of oxygen, nitrogen, and argon. So—such familiar phenomena as light and breath, when we really take them seriously, are much more mysterious than we commonly suppose.

But are the vastness of the universe and the complexity of the atmosphere more baffling really than the birth of a baby or the music of a symphony? You who have stood as proud parents by the bassinet of your sleeping offspring, have you never marveled at the mysteries of reproduction? Distinctive personality emerging from nondescript protoplasm; green eyes, blue eyes, brown eyes, blond hair, brown hair, black hair—all shades and varieties coming out of the same colorless material. Then when you have called that baby "ours," has not the very word made you pause and ponder—in what sense "ours"? To what degree "ours"? For how long "ours"?—causing you to conclude that there is much more to the familiar phenomenon of birth than appears on the surface.

You who have watched that baby become a child, then have walked hand in hand for that first day of school—outwardly speaking glib words of encouragement when all the while a thousand butterflies beat their wings against your breakfast. Have you never paused to marvel at the miracle of growth? Inarticulate sounds becoming spoken language; random muscle thrusts becoming readable writing (well, recognizable anyhow); undirected responses becoming communicable thoughts—causing you to conclude that there is much more to growth than appears on the surface.

You who have found someone to love with admiration and affection, but much more than that, one to whom you deliberately chose to give your fullest allegiance and truest devotion, have you never stood in awe before the mystery of romance, before the fact that one special person could add so many special meanings to your life, causing you to conclude that there is much more to romance than appears on the surface?

You who have sat quietly listening to the labored breathing of one dear to you, expecting every exhalation to be the last. Then one of them is the last! And though you have been waiting for it for hours—and even days—it seems so sudden when breathing stops! Have you not at that moment paused before the *mysterium tremendum* of death, the mystery tremendous, indeed, that this one who just now was with you in your house is now walking in the direction of another room in his Father's house, causing you to conclude that there is much more to death than appears on the surface?

And how often it is, with this sense of awe and wonder before the mysteries of the familiar, that our sense of the sacred has a chance to emerge. Unable adequately to account for or fully to understand the deep dimensions of meaning perceived beneath the surface of things, the worshiper finds himself beginning slowly but surely to move in the direction of a suspicion that there is something or someone high and lifted up above him who can fully account for, and who does adequately understand, these deeper dimensions that are beyond him.

So Moses looks at a flaming bush and responds reverently by removing his shoes to stand on holy ground. Isaiah enters the Temple to mount a throne left empty by the death of his king, only to emerge from the Temple with the vision of a Monarch who never dies. Paul starts down a dusty road to persecute the Christians, only to run headlong into a blinding encounter with Christ that leaves him the advocate of the early Christians. Familiar surroundings take on unfamiliar significance; molehill situations turn into mountain-top experiences.

It is so, even in our time. In language which is more compatible to us than the strange figures of speech used by the founders of our faith, Albert Einstein, after sitting down and pondering mathematical symbols and scientific data, declares: "The most beautiful and most profound emotion we can experience is the sensation of the mystical. It is the source of all true science . . . That deeply emotional conviction of the presence of a superior reasoning power, which is revealed in the incomprehensible universe, forms my idea of God."*

Or even more recently, astronomer Harlow Shapley reports his own deductions from the data available: "The new knowledge

* Philipp Frank, *Einstein: His Life and Time* (New York: Alfred A. Knopf, Inc., 1965), p. 284.

from many sources makes obsolete many of the earlier world views. The new discoveries and developments contribute to the unfolding of a magnificent universe. To be a participant is itself a glory. We are associated in an existence and an evolution that inspire respect and deep reverence. We cannot escape humility."

To stop and wonder, however, is to discover more mysteries than those in the world around us. It is to discover quite as many mysteries in the world within us. The awareness of a plus outside of life that we come to identify with the transcendent, holy God leads our worshiping minds on to a heightened awareness of a deeper dimension within ourselves.

Dr. Richard Cabot, former professor at Harvard Medical School, used to like to point out that one of the tricks of fortune tellers was to emphasize these deep dimensions of potential in each person. He was convinced that it was a favorite trick with those who pretended to read the palm of the hand to observe with special emphasis and secrecy to each customer that they could see in the hand that the deepest and best of the customer had not yet found expression. Half unconsciously he was repressing a flood of power which pushed ever for freedom. To set that power free would be the deepest joy of the customer's life. Dr. Cabot viewed the beauty of this ever-successful trick as residing in the fact that what the fortune teller pretended to discover in each individual he knew full well to be true of every living being.

Of course. All of us are much more than we have ever yet become. Our chronic temptation is not so much to overestimate our problems as to underestimate our powers. Our very folk phrases pay tribute to this fact. Who has never said after some exacting experience, "I didn't know I had it in me"? But that stamina, that patience, that understanding, that courage, that forgiveness that was pulled out of you by a crisis situation had been in you potentially all the while. Again, who has never said about another or heard it said of himself, "Thank goodness, he has at last found himself!" What is meant by that? We mean that that person who has for years been playing around with his fragmentary self has now encompassed his whole self.

Yet this more that is within each human being is a qualitative consideration as well as quantitative. It is not just that you as an individual have a capacity for growth that is much greater than you have ever realized, but that your reach toward the fulfillment of your potential is of cosmic significance, just because you are you, and nobody else is you. To paraphrase the popular song: This universe wants to be loved by you, affirmed by you, just because it can never be affirmed by anyone else as you affirm it.

The fingerprint has been our traditional tribute paid to this factor of individuality. But these days geneticists are telling us that our individuality is much more extensive than that. They keep telling us that we are distinguishably ourselves, not just as far as our fingerprints, but all over. Some of them insist that just a bit of human flesh will be enough to identify the individual, because uniqueness cannot be lost. The individual sex and coloring and the general appearance of the individual will be the easiest features to sort out. The explanation is that in each member in every species difference in pigmentation, body shape, features, blood types, and many other traits result from special combinations of genes; and these produce distinctive types of chemical compounds detectable under analysis of even a minute sample. This, then, is a part of the mystery that you encounter within yourself—a self that is at the same time touched with the infinite, yet distinctively individual; that has about it many aspects that are universal, but is at the same time unique.

We said at the outset that the surest way to nourish our sense of the sacred was to stop and wonder about three things—not only the mysteries around us, and the mysteries within us, but also the relationship between the two. And what is that relationship? The plus outside us that we have learned in our heritage to call the transcendent, holy God appears to have placed a binding claim upon the plus inside us that we have chosen to call God's image! God has given us the freedom to be prodigals but has not given us the freedom to cease to be sons. Even when we are prodigals—we are prodigal sons. Or, as Rufus Jones used to quote the little boy who complained to his mother, "Mom, I've got something inside me I can't do what I want to with." In that complaint the boy was giving a definition of what Rufus Jones meant by conscience. That is definition enough for us. So, we encounter that which not only encounters us but also claims us. The central affirmation of our heritage is that the something inside us we can't do what we want to with is the God in us being claimed in covenant relationship by the God beyond us.

One of the most helpful descriptions of this inescapable relationship between the divine within and the divine without was given in an article written by Bonaro Overstreet. She was reporting an episode that had occurred during one of her midwestern lectures. In the question period that followed her address, one question was asked that she began to answer much too quickly.

"I got so involved," she said, "in defending my own pride instead of that of the questioner that without seeing quickly enough where my words were taking me, I put the asker on the spot and I made the question that he had given sound silly. As soon as it happened I knew I had mangled both an intellectual process and a human relationship. I had a strong feeling of having let down something far greater than myself. I had done damage to human relationships, to human brotherhood, to the principle of love, to the God-in-man, if you will, and at one of the points where I was privileged to choose a way of action and to exert an influence.

"This awareness of failure is, I believe," said Bonaro Overstreet, "a part and parcel of the religious sense of stewardship. If you feel that something has been entrusted to your care, then the sense of shortcoming cannot become a dead-end anxiety about the self.

Both the nature of our failure and the degree of it are measured by a larger yardstick—by what we responsibly take to be true about men and the universe."*

What a haunting phrase! "Measured by a larger yardstick." Our actions measured, not just by the yardstick of our personal whims or social mores, but by the yardstick of something that has the dimension of eternity. Yet have you not, like Bonaro Overstreet, on occasion felt your own actions probed by some such standard? If you have not, then do not pretend that you have. There is no good in that. But if you have, then let's not pretend you have not.

When you have performed in an ugly fashion, have you ever felt that you have mutilated not just one relationship but the canvas of creative beauty itself? When you have deceived, have you ever felt that you have violated not just your own integrity but the integrity of the universe—the foundation of truth on which all relationships must rest? When you have been cruel or petty, unkind or pompous, have you ever had the feeling that your behavior has disturbed, not just the circumference that you can reach with your arms, but the whole orbit of man's life and meaning? Well, to have any of these feelings is, like Bonaro Overstreet, to have to face up to the full dimension of your guilt and your regret.

Long years ago St. Augustine described the yardstick in terms of a God Who made us for Himself and Who leaves us restless until we rest in Him. More recently, for a mechanical age, the late C. S. Lewis used to refer to the God Who designed the human machine to run on Himself and therefore it failed to operate on any other kind of fuel. But why be so negative?

We began this meditation by referring to several who did not konk out. Moses led his people out of Egypt. Isaiah prophesied from the city wall. Paul carried the gospel to two continents. Yes, and much more at the level at which you and I are likely to operate, Bonaro Overstreet wrote a letter of apology to the man whom she

* From "Guilt Feelings: Creative and Uncreative" in *Pastoral Psychology*, May 1955, vol. 6, p. 18.

had offended. As a consequence, she was able to write a conclusion to her experience.

"There was a final aspect of this guilt experience of mine that seems to be religious though I find it hard to define. When I had written my apology and the man's generous answer had come, I felt a curious flood of peace and gratitude. As nearly as I can describe it, it was a sense of homecoming. By my own ineptitude and unkindness and my prideful defense of my own mistake I had put myself outside the value system in which I believe. It was a chill and restless place to be. By writing my letter I had, so to speak, knocked slyly on the door and it was opened unto me. It was opened by the simple warm responsiveness of a fellow human being; but the peace into which I entered was larger than the peace of any single human relationship. It was the great peace of life's having been affirmed rather than denied."*

The excuse for this meditation is that you and I live in a time in which the pressures upon us all, whatever age, all too readily bend us to permit ourselves to live outside the system of values in which we really do believe. It is a chill and restless place to be. The one way forward toward fulfillment is to knock gently on the door, in whatever form is appropriate, and to find our way back to that sense of homecoming that is ours when we are in tune with the highest values that have claimed us. For the transcendent, holy God we encounter in the mysteries around us has placed a binding claim upon the image of God that He has placed within us. To fight that claim is to feel life's tearing tension. To affirm that claim is to move toward life's ultimate meaning.

---

* Bonaro Overstreet, *ibid.*, pp. 21-22.

Two

BEING TOUGH-MINDED AND

WHOLE-HEARTED

"Test everything; hold fast to what is good . . ."

ONE OF the newer organizations in the greater Los Angeles area is a Conference on Science and Religion. Its stated purpose is "to share the common ground between science and religion in search of a deeper meaning for existence." According to a publication of the conference, the dynamic that gives life to its work and makes its ministry viable in the midst of so many other organizations is suggested by these lines of Kahlil Gibran: "Your reason and your passion are the rudder and the sail of your seafaring soul. If either your sail or your rudder be broken, you can but toss and drift or else be held at a standstill in midseas. For reason ruling alone is a force confining; and passion, unattended, is a flame that burns to its own destruction."*

* Kahlil Gibran, *The Prophet* (New York: Alfred A. Knopf, Inc., 1960), p. 50.

of a few years back who insisted that members of the present generation seeing Jesus walking on the water would not respond by saying, "My Lord and My God!" Rather, they would respond by sincerely suggesting—and with admiration—"Say, man, do that over again. I didn't catch how you did it!" And that honest approach to truth is, I submit, the essence of reverence.

But we ask not only—is it factually true?—but also is it functionally true? Does it really work the way those who commend it say that it works? Does it do for the person what he has a right to expect it to do for him on the basis of a clear understanding of its proper function? I often suggest to seminary classes on preaching that it is a good thing there isn't a Pure Food and Drug Act that applies to preachers and their glowing pronouncements from the pulpits, because if there were, many of us would be behind prison bars, unable as we often are to deliver "as advertised." This functional test is legitimately applied to everything preachers claim as well as everything anybody else claims.

Tom and Jenny Harris, agricultural missionaries in Borneo, are betting their lives on the validity of the functional approach to truth and its authenticating power. Soon after they went to Borneo they wrote back to friends about the serious damage being done to their corn crops by destructive beetles. As soon as the beetles arrived, in keeping with the hoary tradition of their ancestors, the natives took a handful of the pests, put them on a barge, and rowed them down the river. That was supposed to destroy the rest of the beetles. It didn't. The spray that Tom Harris used proved to be much more effective than the old method. Why? Because the spray had been prepared with a much closer relationship to that which is really true about beetles!

It is precisely this pragmatic test we must constantly be applying to the styles of life imposed upon us or suggested to us or practiced among us. What if waging war to keep peace, what if surfeiting ourselves with gadgets in an effort to feel significant, what if attempting to achieve brotherhood within the structures of prejudice and segregation, what if each one of these at long last should prove to be as ancient and ineffective a superstition about the way things really work as floating beetles on a barge to protect corn crops? In that case, you see, what we desperately need are not fewer but more and different truths if we are really to be set free.

In testing everything, of course, we need to ask at least one other question. Not only is it factually true and is it functionally true, but also, is it true in any ultimate sense? Suppose it does work in the way it is supposed to work—does it really make any difference? Does it matter?

Back in the days when the installation of telephone lines all the way from the east coast to the state of Texas was completed, a celebration was held. One of the speakers, quite excited about the significance of the day, in his oration exclaimed, "It is now possible for a man in Boston to talk to a man in Dallas!" Whereupon some Thoreauish individual in the crowd upset the applecart on the occasion by asking, "But suppose the man in Boston doesn't have anything to say to the man in Dallas?" There is your ultimate test of truth—the value test. Does it matter? In the scale of personal values, how significant is it?

Nels Ferré reports that in his naïve, boyish days as a student, he once asked the great philosopher Alfred North Whitehead if he could summarize reality in one sentence. Instead of cutting him down for his impudence and naïve approach (as Ferré says he now realizes Whitehead might well have done), Professor Whitehead answered Ferré's question by summarizing reality in one sentence —"It matters, and it has consequences."

So—those of us who would celebrate the excitement of staying open to God's truths will test everything. We will be persistently asking, "Is it factually true? Does it correspond with, or at least not contradict, the known data of experience? Is it functionally true? Does it work? And third, and most important, is it ultimately true? Does it really matter and does it have ultimate consequences?"

But this first letter to embryonic Christians, admonishing them

Being Tough-minded and Whole-hearted

to learn to use their reason and to harness their passions, carried a two-part approach. The first part was the recommendation to test everything. The second part was just as important as the first; hold fast to what is good. And why the second admonition? Because in the "feeding of one's mind with the truths of God," there are two temptations at opposite extremes. The first temptation is to swallow everything without chewing—that is the package deal, the all-or-nothing approach of the dogmatist. But the second temptation is to go on forever chewing but never swallowing. And this is the approach of the cynic, the skeptic, the pseudointellectual. The first results in bloating, the second in malnutrition.

Holding fast to what is good is a demonstrable principle of progress in every realm. The way to move toward what is better is to bet our lives on the best we have yet discovered and verified up to this time. The purest research scientist does exactly that. My image of the scientist is not, in fact, the image of a man of ice-water objectivity. Rather, I think of a scientist as a person who is passionately committed to disinterested inquiry. But the passionate commitment is quite as important as the disinterested inquiry. It is only because he has committed his heart to the superior worth, for him, of objective and disinterested inquiry that the scientist uses his head for just such objective research. In method, he is a man of facts. In motive and mission, he is a man of faith. Like all of the rest of us, he moves out into the vast areas of the unknown on the wings of the best that he has yet come to believe. So we test our faith by facts; but we extend our facts through faith. So true is this, indeed that a not inappropriate motto to be engraved over each laboratory would be: "Ye Must Have Faith."

Many scientific achievements, such as lunar landings and exploration, demonstrate this truth in as eloquent a way as we could hope. Some years ago now we passed the point at which the wingspread of the commercial planes being constructed was greater than the total distance traveled by the first plane the Wright brothers developed. Now we have realized in fact what was formerly only science-fiction fantasy—landing men on the moon—though we still are looking for a cure for the common cold!

How did we move this tremendous distance in so short a time? We are on the threshold of changing what seemed to be fantasy into fact because some people made a passionate commitment of faith. The Wright brothers held fast to the best that they were able to sift from the many sources of information and the contradictory and conflicting theories that were available to them about flying heavier-than-air machines. Building on those discernible facts, and having faith that there were more facts yet to be discovered, they and others bet their lives in such a way that we are now on the threshold where we stand. So progress in individual morality and social ethics, in personal responsibility and in the community of caring, come through the same working principles. We are going to be able to move closer to more truth than we yet claim by holding fast to the best truths we already know.

Charles Lindbergh abstracted thus and reported his resolution to use his passion in the direction he felt life was meant to go in his autobiography, *Of Flight and Life.* And it is important to remember as you read that Charles Lindbergh's journey through life included the loss of a baby son who was kidnapped and killed. Yet on one page he called "My Greatest Discovery" he wrote:

> To me in youth science was more important than either man or God. I worshiped science. I was awed by its knowledge. Its advances had surpassed man's wildest dreams. In its learning seemed to lie the key to all the mysteries of life. It took many years for me to discover that science, with all its brilliance, lights only a middle chapter of creation. I saw the science I worshiped and the aircraft I loved destroying the civilization I expected them to serve and which I thought as permanent as earth itself.
>
> Now I realize that to survive one must look beyond the speed and power of aircraft, beyond the material strength of science. And though God cannot be seen as tangibly as I had demanded

Being Tough-minded and Whole-hearted

as a child, His presence can be sensed in every sight and act and incident. Now I know that when a man loses this sense (of Presence) he misses the true quality of life—the beauty of the earth, its seasons and its skies; the brotherhood of men; the joy of wife and children. He loses the infinite strength without which no people can survive—the element which war cannot defeat or peace corrupt.

Now I understand that spiritual truth is more essential to a nation than the mortar in its cities' walls. For when the actions of the people are unguided by these truths, it is only a matter of time before the walls themselves collapse.

The most urgent mission of our time is to understand these truths, and to apply them to our way of modern life. We must draw strength from the almost forgotten virtues of simplicity, humility, contemplation, prayer. It requires a dedication beyond science and beyond self—but the rewards are great and it's our only hope.*

That is Charles Lindbergh's "greatest discovery"!—a sense of Presence. What is yours? What is mine? About what truths of life are we ready to say, "Now I realize, now I understand, now I know. These are the passionate commitments I make on the basis of the best that I have ever come to experience." Whatever they are, this is what I am saying to us: to bet our lives on the best of these truths is our best and only hope for becoming better.

This is a wonderful world in which we live and learn, and learning is one of the most exciting as well as most authentic ways to worship in this world. How can we draw closer to feeding our minds on God's truths? Here at least is a place to begin: to use our heads and to commit our hearts; to chew well before swallowing; but finding that which tastes like truth to us, for our own soul's growth, to swallow with relish; to test everything; and—having done that—to hold fast to, and to thank God for—the good.

* Charles A. Lindbergh, *Of Flight and Life* (New York: Charles Scribner's Sons, 1948), p. 56.

Three

GETTING OUR IMAGINATIONS

TURNED ON

"O Lord, how manifold are thy works!"
PSALM 104

AT THE peak of the psychedelic movement, I concluded that there was a fundamental truth in the psychedelic contention that vast numbers of people go through this world living out their days and years turned off!—or at best, barely turned on. There are degrees of awareness and dimensions of meaning available to human beings far beyond those that most people ever appropriate. Day after day we live so near to so much, yet claim so little. Like early American Indians gathering twigs for fuel from Pennsylvania hillsides bulging with anthracite coal waiting to be burned, so we have within our reach kindling resources infinitely superior to the impotent substitutes with which we daily try to warm ourselves.

Long before the psychedelics railed against this turned-off condition of so many human beings, the poets complained about

Getting Our Imaginations Turned On

the same thing. Between spasms of coughing caused by terminal tuberculosis, Robert Louis Stevenson wrote his own marching orders for the days left to him, physically crippled though he was:

> *If I have faltered more or less*
> *In my great task of happiness;*
> *If I have moved among my race*
> *And shown no glorious morning face;*
> *If beams from happy human eyes*
> *Have moved me not; if morning skies,*
> *Books, and my food, and summer rain*
> *Knocked on my sullen heart in vain:—*
> *Lord, thy most pointed pleasures take*
> *And stab my spirit broad awake; . . .**

Before Stevenson and the other poets entered their complaints, the world's most viable religions were quite as opposed to any turned-off condition of human beings. Most of them avowedly set themselves to the correction of this condition. Spokesman for Zen Buddhism in this country across recent years have explained the objective of their popular movement in just such fashion. Their word is that Zen is aimed at those who die of hunger while sitting beside the rice bag.

The Old and New Testaments of the Bible are filled with this same theme running through them as a conspicuous thread. "The hearing ear and the seeing eye, the Lord has made them both," says the Book of Proverbs. Repeatedly, from other writers in the Bible, comes the lament for those, "who, having eyes, see not"; "having ears, hear not"; and "having hearts, harden those hearts against me."

How many of the distinctions of the New Testament between "lost and found," "darkness and light," "life and death" are improvisations on this same theme. Just as modern medicine makes

---

* Robert Louis Stevenson, "The Celestial Surgeon" from *Underwoods* (New York: Charles Scribner's Sons, 1887).

much not just of "sickness" and of "health," but of "degrees of wellness"—so our New Testament makes much not just of "life" or "death," but of "degrees of aliveness"! "This my son was dead," said the father of the Prodigal, "but now he is alive!" Did he mean that his son had physically died and been resurrected into physical life? Of course not. He meant that through the grace of the "turned-on imagination" his son had come alive to dimensions of meaning and qualities of relationship he had never before assumed.

The iniative of such grace is, of course, with God. A fundamental assumption of our religion is that precisely the operation that Robert Louis Stevenson asks of the "Celestial Surgeon," God performs twenty-four hours of every day. All the days of our years, God seeks "to stab our spirits broad awake" with His pointed pleasures. He carpets the mountain meadows with wild flowers and stocks the riffled streams with rainbow trout. He greets the dawn with a symphony of birdsong and punctuates the night with a sunset radiance. He permeates the air with the fragrance of roses and perforates the skies with the glittering of stars. Yet, in spite of all, for some of us it does seem that day in and day out, God knocks on our sullen hearts in vain.

One can almost believe that God at times must feel ever so much like that British sailor described in an oft-told story. He dived one day into the waters of Plymouth Harbor and saved the life of a little boy. Three days later the sailor came across the boy and his mother in the streets of Plymouth. He saw the boy nudge his mother, and the mother then stopped the sailor and said, "Are you the young man who pulled my little boy out of Plymouth Harbor the other day?" Expecting some kind of gratitude, the sailor straightened up, smiled, and replied, "Yes, Madam." "Well, then," said the mother with mounting anger, "where's his cap?" Quite like that sullen mother, you and I must seem to God when, so obsessed with our frantic quest for the trivial, we scarcely acknowledge His saving gift of the essential.

Wordsworth watched his own generation make that mistake until, unable to stand it longer, he cried out in rebellion:

> *The world is too much with us, late and soon,*
> *Getting and spending, we lay waste our powers:*
> *Little we see in Nature that is ours;*
> *We have given our hearts away, a sordid boon,*
> *This sea that bares her bosom to the moon,*
> *The winds that will be howling at all hours*
> *And are upgathered now like sleeping flowers;*
> *For this, for everything, we are out of tune*
> *It moves us not . . ."**

And for all too many, even in our day, Wordsworth's words are still pointedly appropriate.

But they need not be. There is no compulsion forcing you and me to parade through life—to use a phrase of Carlyle's—as "a pair of spectacles behind which there are no eyes." We can set outselves to the rewarding business of keeping alive to the beauty about us. And when we do, God's pointed pleasures will keep our spirits alive.

In place of the fears and anxieties that have been haunting our imaginations these pointed pleasures will supply visions of the good and the true and the beautiful to sustain us. We do not pretend to know the full explanation of the healing processes of beauty, but some of its workings are clear to us.

For one, a heightened awareness of the beauty about us can shift our attention from temporary styles to permanent stabilities. A five-year-old son of a close friend put it neatly years ago. He was accompanying his father along a California highway. "Daddy," Danny broke in as they rode along, "how long is it going to be before I can have a car of my own to drive?" Dr. McCall explained

---

* William Wordsworth "The World Is Too Much With Us" in *The World's Great Religious Poetry*, edited by Caroline Mills Hill (New York: The Macmillan Company, 1923), pp. 248-49.

that as soon as he was old enough legally and proved himself responsible, he could have a car of his own. "But, Danny," he continued, "by the time you are old enough to drive a car, maybe we won't even be buying you a car at all. Maybe we will be buying you an airplane instead, or maybe a combination airplane and car. For you see, Danny, in fifteen years or so, the design in cars will probably have changed a lot."

Danny was silent. As they rode along, he gazed out of the window. Finally, he broke the silence, "Well, Daddy, don't you think in fifteen years the design of everything will be changed—except the bushes?" "Thus," said Dr. McCall, "scripture was fulfilled. My little child led me to a vivid realization that man's designs are always changing, but God's designs are eternal."

I strongly suspect that you and I need to have that scripture fulfilled in our lives. Life moves at such a rapid pace. For any one of us to go back over the calendar of even his last few years is to find a record of changes so numerous and drastic as to be almost unbelievable. Try it out and see for yourself. Call the roll of your family. Get out the old photograph albums of your friends. Parade the past before you in any manner you choose. The panorama of change will flash with such rapidity and extension that, unless you shift your focus, you will find your imagination haunted by the dread thought that there is nothing to life but change.

That is just the time for you to go out to see or to hear something beautiful. In the darkest days of 1914 Viscount Grey is reputed to have done just that. When it seemed the First World War had left no light in any sky, he went to Lady Glen Conner's home where Campbell McInnes sang some of Handel's songs. Afterwards Grey expressed the faith to Mr. McInnes that even though Europe was in the most terrible trouble it had ever known in civilized times, and no one could say what would be left in the end, he was quite sure that Handel's music would survive.

Henry F. Lyte had the same sort of wisdom when his physician told him that he was suffering from a malady which was soon going to prove fatal. The story is that after conducting his final Communion Service in the church at Brixham, England, where he had served his people for twenty-four years, he walked through the garden behind his manse down to the seashore. There beside the ever-restless waves but eternal tide, he worked out the imagery and many of the lines of his ever-familiar and famous hymn,

> *Abide with me; fast falls the eventide*
> *The darkness deepens; Lord, with me abide!*

Then into the second stanza of that hymn, he worked the imagery of the insight he was gaining there beside the sea:

> *Change and decay in all around I see;*
> *O Thou who changest not, abide with me.*

For you and me it may not be Handel's music, or the seashore. It may be old Half Dome in Yosemite or the Redwoods along the coast. It may be an aria from some great opera, a copy of a masterpiece, or the twinkle of a star. But whatever it is, there must be, and there can be for each one of us, something or many things to which we can go and from which we can return refreshed, having experienced the beauty and inspiration of something that shifts our attention from man-made styles that are temporary, to God-made stabilities that are eternal. It will be something that enables us to come away singing,

> *Change and decay in all around I see,*
> *O Thou who changest not, abide with me.*

But just because God's pointed pleasures can shift our attention from styles to stabilities, they also serve to purge our imaginations from their obsessions with problems that need to be solved and remind us instead of powers that wait to be used.

In a direct sense, pointed pleasures are themselves sources of just such powers. Color, for example, is known to have a healing value. The frequency of suicides from a London bridge is reported to have been dramatically reduced when the color of the bridge was changed from a dull gray to red. The ladies have known this healing value of color all their lives. For years they have bought those colorful hats and clothes, just to build up their morale. The one difficulty is that when the bills come in something seems to happen to father's morale—and it is not a buildup!

Just so the melody and rhythm of music have a known healing value, too. Long before my good friend, the late Mrs. Wilhelmina Harbert, of the Music Department of the University of the Pacific began her pioneer work in music therapy among mental patients, "Little David" played on his harp to lure King Saul back into a rational state of mind.

Long ago tired slaves with sore, bare feet looked down with wistful eyes at those feet that had never touched shoes and forgot their old problems and found new powers as they softly sang:

> *I got shoes, you got shoes,*
> *All God's chillun got shoes;*
> *When I get to heav'n*
> *Gwine put on dem shoes—*
> *Gwine walk all over God's heav'n.*

Yes, and not so long ago the eldest daughter among five children in a Methodist parsonage with which I happened to have been closely acquainted used to come home from school and head directly for the piano. The rest of the family never bothered to ask how the day had gone. They just listened to her play. As long as she hammered at some passage from Chopin's "Polonaise" they knew enough to steer clear of the front room. But, by the time she eased off into something like a Brahm's "Lullaby," they figured it was safe to approach her.

The God-appointed pleasures of color and rhythm and natural wonder serve as symbols as well as sources of useable power. Listen to a forest ranger tell the thrilling story of an 1,800-year-old giant redwood that has been felled and a slice preserved. Here in this wooden tree ring is evidence of blight. This year's ring indicates that a great fire swept through. Another ring tells of a serious drought. And as you listen, fill your imagination with the thought that you, too, like that redwood, have recuperative powers. God has placed tremendous resiliency within human beings as well as in natural beings such as trees.

Listen again to the parable of the pearl. Note how the oyster treats that grain of sand or other foreign matter that has penetrated its shell as an irritation. Unable to eliminate the intruder, the oyster proceeds to assimilate it. So it transforms the irritation into a beautiful pearl. As you ponder the pearl, fill your imagination with the knowledge that God offers you the same creative power to transform unwanted experiences of your life into sources of growth and radiance.

Or, look on the murky waters of the marsh while the tide is out—as ugly a sight as you will ever see. But then look again when the eternal tide has come in and lifted the weeds out of the mud and filled the ditches with water. Then with a sense of burden upon you perhaps as great as Sidney Lanier felt as he looked upon the marshes of Glynn and battled tuberculosis in an advanced stage, see as he did in the lifting power of the tide a symbol of God's undergirding power:

As the marsh hen secretly builds on the watery sod,
Behold I will build me a nest on the greatness of God.

Having let God's pointed pleasures shift your attention from styles to stabilities and from problems to powers, may you let those same pointed pleasures shift your attention from the barriers that keep us apart to the bonds that unite.

The realms of beauty, of aesthetics, of the arts can fill our imaginations with the understanding that our seeming differences are but a part of a significant unity. One of the college boys put it aptly one day when he stood up at the University of the Pacific and said at a pep rally, "I am a Roman Catholic from Southern California, and the first class I have every morning is Hebrew

The Power of Worship

Heritage!" That is the way life is meant to be. Because that is the way life achieves its highest unity and greatest beauty.

If we watch it in the realm of art forms, we will discover that is true. Rests as well as beats are needed to produce rhythm. Clouds as well as light are indispensable to a sunset. Life at its best uses its powers, not in isolation, but in combination.

A beautiful church is a perfect illustration of this point. It is a demonstration of what happens when the artists and the artisans, the mechanics and the musicians, the glass blowers and the masons combine their talents and energies.

It is no accident that moonlight and roses, lavender and old lace, buttons and bows have always been a part of the process of falling in love. For the first part of falling in love is drawing close together, and an essential part of drawing close together is the sharing of life's lovelies.

Neither is it any accident that our destructive prejudices are most readily laid aside in the presence of someone who demonstrates a talent for increasing the pointed pleasures of life through the art forms of music, or painting, or drama, or writing. Only a bigot could fail to appreciate Harry Belafonte's singing because he is a Negro; Andre Kostelanetz's conducting because he is a Russian; Jascha Heifetz's violin playing because he is a Jew; or Evelyn Waugh's novels because he is a Roman Catholic.

If we give ourselves half a chance, God's pointed pleasures can open our eyes to the fact that melody has no nationality, talent is color-blind, and beauty is creedless. The values that really do abide and the powers that really do sustain are the monopoly of no man, no nation, no race, no creed. They are every man's heritage because they really do belong to Him—to the God of all men—by whom every good and perfect gift is given.

But in addition to realizing through the beauty around us that the artists and artisans, in spite of all their differences, actually work better together, we come as well to understand that just so—the human and the divine, in spite of the diversities that seem to separate them, actually have bonds that pull them together, too. This discovery brings us at last to the point of understanding that Bliss Carman sings for us all when in "Vestigia" he reports an experience of his which can be ours:

I took a day to search for God,
And found Him not. But as I trod
By rocky ledge, through woods untamed,
Just where one scarlet lily flamed
I saw His footprint in the sod.

Then suddenly, all unaware,
Far off in the deep shadows, where
A solitary hermit thrush
Sang thru the holy twilight hush—
I heard His voice upon the air.

And even as I marveled how
God gives us heaven here and now.
In a stir of wind that hardly shook
The poplar leaves beside the book—
His hand was light upon my brow.

At last with evening as I turned
Homeward, and thought what I had learned
And all that there was still to probe
I caught the glory of His robe,
Where the last fires of sunset burned.

(And so)—
Back to the world with quickened start
I looked and longed for any part
In making saving beauty be . . .
And from that kindling ecstasy
I knew God dwelt within my heart.*

---

* "Vestigia" by Bliss Carman in *The World's Great Religious Poetry*, edited by Caroline Mills Hill (New York: The Macmillan Company, 1923), p. 32.

Four

ENCOUNTERING GOD AS A

FOUR-LETTER WORD

"If God is for us, who can be against us!"

ROMANS 8:31

THE GREAT educator Horace Mann once stumped his home state of Massachusetts pleading for the establishment of a welfare home for children. At one point in the campaign he became so enthusiastic for the project that he was moved to exclaim, "This home would be worth all the money in the treasury of the state of Massachusetts if it should save only one boy!" Whereupon one opponent to the project cracked back, "Aren't you making that a little too strong?" "No," exclaimed Horace Mann in reply, "not if it were my boy!"

Our religious heritage has been trying to say precisely this across the centuries about the love of God. We cannot make it too strong or state it too extravagantly. All of us are "God's boys" and all of us are "God's girls." We are all God's children. So valuable are we in his sight that He will use all the resources consistent with His nature to help us sense his presence, to appropriate satisfactions and to actualize the best and the most of our own potential.

What is more, God's love is not conditional love. It is not something that through great effort we can earn from God. It is something that with great eagerness God offers us. The Apostle Paul said it in that familiar line of his. So intense is this love that nothing, from God's side, can ever separate us from his love. Indeed, "If God is for us, who can be against us!" And the central message of the gospel is that God is for us. That, in fact, is what the four-letter word "love" means: the forces of this universe are supportive of what we are intended to be and to become. The Power that holds the planets in their places is the Love that will not let us go.

It would seem, therefore, having been cradled in such a heritage, as most of us have quite literally been, that one of the simplest tricks of our lives would be to manage that exciting aspect of worship in this wonderful world that Archbishop William Temple referred to as "opening our hearts to the love of God." Yet many of us, in our honest moments, are quick to reply that to believe in and to respond to such love is one of the most difficult of accomplishments. That there is Mind in back of this vast universe many of us find relatively easy to believe. That there is a design, a discernible purpose of some creative sort running through all this complex activity—many of us are able to assent to. But that there is a personal concern for each one of us on the part of the Creative Source that is back of this universe—that is what most of us find it hardest of all to accept.

For some of us, philosophically or academically inclined, such a concept at times seems so incredible as to amount to an absurdity. Others of us more emotionally biased toward life are so offended by the appalling pain and massive suffering around us that such a concept of God as love seems so contradictory as to amount to an obscenity. Stendahl has spoken this in a pointed epigram. Condemning the massive pain and suffering in life, he exclaimed, "The only excuse for God is that He does not exist!"

But what about those of us who still support the notion that the Power that holds the planets in their places is the Love that will not let us go is neither an absurdity nor an obscenity but bedrock reality? How do we go about aligning ourselves with such reality?

A little boy by the name of Martin outlines the answer in his childish prayer. You may have seen it published in your newspaper. It read:

> *Dear God:*
> *My father is mean.*
> *Please get him not to be.*
> *But don't hurt him.*
> *Sincerely,*
> *Martin**

Confronting a life full of meanness as it is, and yet responding with an affirmation of life carried to the point of wanting to help rather than to hurt, Martin personalizes the way to open our hearts to the love of God.

To begin with, quite like Martin we can never open our hearts with our heads; and there is no use to try. We can argue our heads off but we cannot argue our hearts open to God's love.

In this the love of God is like almost everything else in the realm of values. Take music, for instance. Try to argue someone who refuses to listen to music into believing that music is beautiful, and see how far you get. Imagine, for example, that when you first heard that Isaac Stern was to open the symphony season in your city this year you invited a friend, who had never heard Isaac Stern play his violin, to share the wonderful evening with you. But, in making the invitation, you discover that through

* "Letters to God," daily feature in *Los Angeles Times*, Nov. 8, 1968.

some freak of environment, your friend has never heard of a violin, much less of Isaac Stern. In other ways he is a true pseudo-scientific son of the twentieth century. That is, he labors under the dual delusion, first, that he is strictly an objective thinker. (If you doubt this in his presence, he will beat on his desk in anger, and his face will get red with rage at your questioning his objectivity.) But, second, he can accept as valid and valuable only that which you can prove to him to be worthwhile on the basis of mathematical precision and logical formula. In keeping with these delusions, your friend insists, therefore, that before he can accept your invitation to hear Isaac Stern, he must first have a complete and convincing analysis of what violin music is really like.

And so you try to explain: "A highly developed form of *Homo sapiens* will stand upon a platform. On his left shoulder, under his first chin, he will place a strange box-like contraption of highly polished wood. Along the handle of that box-like contraption, over a thin piece of wood over a hole in the box, will be stretched four strings of stainless steel and nylon. With his left hand our highly developed form of *Homo sapiens* will press down and up on these four strings, while in his right hand, stretched across a stick about a yard long, something like a yardstick (and the friend must know about that because a yardstick is used for measurement and he is acquainted with measurement), will be hair taken from the tail of a horse. And with that hair taken from the tail of a horse, he will stroke those strings of stainless steel and nylon.

"Accompanying him will be another form of highly developed *Homo sapiens* who will be pressing down with his fingers on black and white keys of ivory that are attached to wooden arms that have on them hammers padded with felt, that will be striking long strings of steel, that are also enclosed in a large box-like contraption. And when those two gentlemen get together, what you hear is something out of this world!" And by that argument you convince your friend that violin music is beautiful—or do you?

Dr. Harry Emerson Fosdick gave the classic answer to that

question long years ago when he used a similar analogy. He pointed out that music, quite like the love of God, is not a proposition to be argued, but a response to be experienced, a relationship to be learned. He said, "We argue religion too much. Vital religion, like good music, needs not defense, but rendition. A wrangling controversy over religion is precisely as if the members of an orchestra should beat the folks over the head with their violins to prove that music is beautiful. But such procedure is no way to prove that music is beautiful. Play it!"

That is what we are saying in the first place about opening our hearts to God's love. We cannot open our hearts with our heads. What then can we use? And, as little Martin illustrates, the answer is to use our necks. We can stick out our necks to life as love, even when our experience includes the contrary evidence that life is also "mean." We can adventure forth into this strange mixture of heartache and happiness using love as the point of reference, the principle of interpretation, by means of which we seek to understand the mysteries, to make our way through the sufferings, and to discover our goal in the midst of detours. We can stay open enough to be vulnerable to the sufferings in order to enable ourselves to be capable of the satisfactions. We do not wait to open our hearts until we are convinced that love is in life; we become convinced that love is in life by opening up our hearts.

What is the necessity for this hazardous approach? It is the fact that in this strange mixture we call life we so often come closest to what we call love in the midst of experiences that from the outside do not look like love at all. If, therefore, we have been waiting to see how much love they contained before we exposed ourselves to them, we never would have entered into them; yet making our way into and through them, in the midst of difficulties and trials, and even temptations, we found that sense of support that did not let us go and a feeling of companionship that was convincing.

You may remember who spoke these lines: "In my young manhood, I had a critical nervous breakdown. It was the most terrifying wilderness I ever traveled through. I dreadfully wanted to commit suicide, but instead I made some of the most vital discoveries of my life." Who said that? The same man I just quoted as having written about the analogy of music and religion—the late Harry Emerson Fosdick—the man whom many clergymen would designate as the most decisive personal influence on the Protestant ministry in the past fifty years. He is the man who said, "I dreadfully wanted to commit suicide." But instead of supplementing that feeling of despair by withdrawing from life, he kept on sticking out his neck, continuing to make himself vulnerable to life's positive satisfactions.

Describing further that particular period of his life, Dr. Fosdick suggested that we are ever so much like the little boy who argued with his mother, "Why are all the vitamins in spinach instead of ice cream where they ought to be?" And Dr. Fosdick answered, "I don't know. Only God knows that. But the fact that we have to face is that the vitamins are in spinach and God often is in the wilderness!"

But thus squarely to seek the fact of love in the raw stuff of life takes the most elemental sort of courage I know anything about. When what we feel most like doing is to withdraw from life and pull our necks in and never again trust anybody or anything because we have been so hurt, it takes sheer courage to move out into life again. It takes the kind of courage demonstrated in what I feel is one of the most eloquent parables of all time, but which parable was written before our eyes in our own time. That is the parable of the Hiroshima Maidens.

You have read of those twenty-five disfigured Japanese girls who years ago came to our country. Victims of modern warfare, they were so scarred by radiation that they were practically outcasts from society. In a movement begun by Norman Cousins, assisted by the Friends, and supported by the medical profession, these girls were brought to this country to be treated through plastic surgery. Can you imagine yourself in their place? I wonder how they felt when the offer was first made. They were to leave the few familiar and secure surroundings left to them, the few people who had come to accept and understand them; and were to come all the way from their country to this country. They were to come to this country that in a military sense was responsible for their disfigurement to put themselves into the hands of strangers and a new culture—in the hope of being healed. How much raw courage it must have taken for these girls to accept such an invitation.

Yet Norman Cousins gave one report on them that ended with one of the most poignant paragraphs I ever read. "Shortly before one of the girls was wheeled into the operating room, she asked an interpreter to give this message to Dr. Barsky. 'Tell Dr. Barsky not to be worried because he cannot give me a new face. I know my scars are very, very bad and I know Dr. Barsky is worried because he thinks I may expect that I will be as I once was. I know that this is impossible; but it does not matter. Something has already healed here inside.' "*

What we are saying is that given a God of love like ours who is neither an absurdity nor an obscenity but a reality, regardless of how many scars you have—if you will go forth sticking your neck out to life as love, somewhere, sometime you will discover that which heals you "here inside" where it really counts.

But one other positive suggestion is reinforced by Martin's example. We open our hearts to God's love not only by sticking out our necks to life as love, but also by holding out our hands with love to life. Today as always the most convincing proof available that God's love is really getting into us is the evidence that God's love is getting through us to others. You and I seem to be so constructed that the only way our hearts can contain love is

* "Interim Report on the Maidens" by Norman Cousins, *Saturday Review*, Oct. 15, 1955.

not as reservoirs but as channels. In order for God's love to come into us, it has to go through us.

There are innumerable ways in which we can communicate such love to the world today. Ministries of physical healing are among the most needed now as always. Terribly scarred and mutilated as they are as victims of war, Vietnamese children have been brought to this country under a program sponsored by the Committee of Responsibility that at least some of their hurts might be healed. And then perhaps through love held out to them, they may be enabled to stay open to a life that they have experienced as mean. You and I have such physical opportunities, day in and day out, to minister to the needs of the underprivileged and dispossessed at home and abroad.

At the same time there are innumerable opportunities for healing at the mental and emotional level. For we are part of a culture that has many conflicts that are nonphysical but are destructive and terribly severe, nonetheless. We are also part of a culture that has become so crassly materialistic that vast numbers of people narcissistically luxuriate in a style of life affluent beyond anything they have ever earned and yet go on day in and day out talking and acting as if they earned it all, thereby feeling justified in keeping it all to and for themselves. How much healing we can give to a world of selfishness like that—by extending the hand of the responsible kind of stewardship Dr. Richard Cabot of Harvard Medical School exemplified throughout his life. His consideration for others and generosity became a legend around the Harvard Medical School. One day somebody asked him to explain it. His answer was simple: "I heard a thrush singing in the early morning in a wet, dark wood, and I knew ever after that song that I could never get even with life!"

We can hold out our hands with reconciling love in the religious bickerings that go on so frequently and in such subtle ways among us. In recent months, I have had the fascinating, exciting privilege of officiating at weddings, first with a Roman Catholic priest, next with a Mormon bishop, and most recently with a Jewish rabbi. Following the latter ceremony, the rabbi and I were both tremendously impressed by the number of people who came up thanking us for the experience they had just shared. Some of them were undoubtedly impressed by the novelty of it. But many more talked of many more profound meanings. Throughout the ceremony we had emphasized the fact that this was not a reduction to a least common denominator, but an effort to maintain individual integrity; to reverence each other's reverences; and at the same time to move in a dimension of reconciliation as full-orbed human beings. It was this deeper spirit that caught hold of young as well as old—or I should say old as well as young— since the older were even more threatened by what might seem to be disregard for tradition. In a time when overt signs and strong feelings of conflict are so pervasive, an experience of reconciliation, of drawing together, came as a relief; and people responded to it in that spirit.

Or again, we can hold out our hands with the same sort of love to life Dr. Wilfred Grenfell extended over years in Labrador. A great contemporary of Dr. Albert Schweitzer, Dr. Grenfell's first line of ministry was as a medical missionary. But at all times he ministered as well to all the needs of his people. One of the Labrador stories was of a call he received one day from a fishing boat off the coast. Answering their distress signal, he went out and found on that fishing boat an eighteen-year-old girl who had shipped aboard as a cook. Quite unknown to the rest of the crew, she had given premature birth to a baby and, unattended, had fallen into a critical condition. By the time Dr. Grenfell reached her, the best he could do was too little to save her. Realizing that, after doing everything he possibly could medically, he began speaking to her tenderly of one who said, "Come unto me all ye that labor and are heavy laden and I will give you rest." And, said the Doctor, "She found that peace which passeth understanding.

Then," he added, "we laid her tenderly away on a headland jutting out into the Atlantic. And from its summit you could see across the restless waters. On the grave, I planted a rude wooden cross on which we carved these compassionate words of Jesus, 'Neither do I condemn thee.' "

In a day when there are so many ready to condemn everything and everybody, what great good you and I can do for our exciting but weary world by stretching out our hands with just a little bit of love translated into that forgiving spirit.

Little Martin managed it:

> *Dear God:*
> *My father is mean*
> *Please get him not to be.*
> *But don't hurt him.*
> *Sincerely,*
> *Martin*

And we can manage it too. We can open our hearts to God's love—not by arguing our heads off, but by sticking our necks out to life as love, and by holding our hands out with love to life.

Five

DOING OUR THING

"God works through different men in different ways
but it is the same God who achieves his purposes
through them all."

I CORINTHIANS 12:4–5 (Phillips translation)

IN THE sight of God nobody is anybody compared with others.
Everybody is somebody in his own right. God cares quite as much
for the peddler as for the Pope, for the mechanic as for the monk,
for the anonymous riveter on the assembly line as for the Holly-
wood star whose name is on every marquee. In the pattern of
providence, every person is important—so important that God
makes each one of us the object of his unconditional love. But so
important as well, God makes each one of us a partner in his
eternal purpose.

The Apostle Paul said it, "God works through different men
in different ways, but it is the same God who achieves his purposes through them all." In the sight of God nobody is anybody
compared with others. Everybody is somebody in his own right.
All of which sounds innocent enough as a generalization, but it

explodes with the force of dynamite whenever we implement it as a working principle in our daily lives. See what it says about the final aspect of a new world of awareness through worship that Archbishop Temple refers to as "devoting our wills to God's purpose."

For one startling thing, it says that God needs us as much as we need God. If in the pattern of providence God seeks to achieve his purposes through persons, then God needs us to achieve his purposes. Without us, can God accomplish in us and through us what he seeks to accomplish?

The answer depends, of course, on the answer to the other question as to what we think God is trying to accomplish in us and through us. According to the prophets of our Hebrew heritage, the Christ of Christian tradition, and an abundance of supporting evidence from the behavioral sciences, God wants us to love him with our whole selves and to love others as we love ourselves. That, in the jargon of religion and theology, is the supreme purpose which God is trying to accomplish in us and through us. We are to be enabled to will the well-being of the whole being of each being, and thus to achieve the will of the Supreme Being. He wants us to relate freely and affirmatively to life, personally and compassionately to people, intimately and confidently to him. Dr. Albert Outler of Perkins School of Theology summarizes this concept of the purpose of God in the sentence—"God begins the creation as a deliberate venture in developing a community of finitely free creatures capable of blessedness and of sharing in his infinite love."

But the community of love is an affirmative relationship for which we must volunteer. We can never be drafted for love even by God. This supreme purpose God seeks most of all to achieve is the one purpose he cannot achieve alone. He wants a family of children who, finitely free as they are, nevertheless affirm their Father and accept their brothers, not out of necessity but out of choice. Free as they are to lie, they devote themselves to the pursuit of truth; though free to be unfair, they scrupulously seek justice; though free to turn inward narcissistically upon themselves, they turn outward instead in quest of ever-deepening companionships, human and divine.

This kingdom of love is the supreme purpose which God seeks ever to work in his world through persons. As long as we are persons, this is the purpose God seeks to work in and through us. It follows, therefore, that we have copyrighted contributions to make to God's kingdom of character and to this community of voluntary lovers of God and of our fellow man. Unlike our government, God does not issue every order in multiple copies. We are originals for which there are no carbons. We are players for whom there are no substitutes sitting on the bench. If we miss our unique, one-and-only assignments in the time and place allotted to us, there is no one to pick up our assignment for us. Each has his own assignment to pick up for himself. God not only wants to work something in us, then, but God also seeks to work something distinctive for his world through us. The achievement of the supreme purpose of God requires the costly combination of his energies and man's efforts. In the jargon of the day, God cannot do his thing unless we do our thing.

As soon as we say that God needs us as much as we need God, another startling realization dawns upon us: God needs them as much as he needs us; them, those other than we, those different from us; those whose "thing" is quite distinctively other than "our thing." Paul said it, "God works through different persons in different ways to achieve his purposes in the world." In the pattern of providence, differences are not just desirable—they are indispensable. Black is beautiful, and so is brown, and so is red and yellow, and so is white. It takes more than one color and more than one creed, more than one craft and more than one art, more than one talent and more than one temperament to produce this kingdom of loving relationships that we are designating as the supreme purpose of God. In a scheme of things, then, in which differences are not only desirable but necessary, comparisons become not only odious but superfluous; in fact, downright irrelevant. If hydrogen and oxygen are both indispensable to the creation of water, what a waste of time to argue over which is more important when each is indispensable. If a chain is no stronger than its weakest link, how silly to quibble over which link is most important when the chain breaks if any link gives way.

Yet what a devilish time you and I do have, trying to practice this principle of the appreciation of differences. Paul used the analogy of the body. He said, "After all, why should the eye say to the ear, 'I have no need for you?' " We might use the analogy of a university faculty, the English department saying to the physical education department, "I have no need for you." Or the drama department saying to the music department, "I have no need for you." Or we might move over to the realm of medicine, where, I am told, some specialists tell the general practitioner, "I have no need for you."

It almost seeems as if we cannot feel important at all unless we can feel all-important. And that is too bad. Because, as Paul again reminds us, "If the body were all ear, what would we do for seeing?" Just so, if the family of mankind were all musicians, even musicians who sing beautifully for their supper, who would provide the food? Or, if they were all farmers, who would produce the music? Or, if worst came to worst and they were all preachers, then who would practice these preachments we preachers so piously make? If in the family we were all children, who would be the baby-sitters? Or, if we were all adults, who would supply the joy?

Trinity College in Hartford, Connecticut, must have had someone on its staff who had an eloquent appreciation for the contribution of differences. Whenever there was an event in the life of that college that seemed of special significance, that small New England school commemorated the event by carving some symbol of it on the end of one of the chapel pews.

A score of years ago, Trinity College had a football player who was named All-American. That was a special event worthy of commemoration. So they carved a symbol of this event on the end of one of the pews in the chapel. But when the figure was unveiled, everyone was startled. Instead of the All-American crashing over the goal line they had expected to see, the carved figure depicted a third-stringer huddled on the bench with a blanket pulled over his head. He was not the All-American, but without *him* there would have been no All-American!

There is an old saying, "Pygmies on the shoulders of giants see more than the giants." The awful temptation for pygmies, therefore, is to begin to feel bigger than the giants. So, sons on the shoulders of fathers may sometimes see more than fathers. But it always behooves the sons to remember the special vantage point which makes possible their favorable perspective. This is one son who would like ever to bear witness, therefore, to the broad elevation of the shoulders from which he has been privileged to view the world.

G. K. Chesterton is credited with pointing up the practical implications of this appreciation of the contributions to be made through our differences. The story describes his sitting with a group discussing the question, "If you were cast up on a deserted island and could have only one book for your encouragement, what would it be?" One fellow said, "I would like the Bible." Another member said he would like to have Shakespeare's plays. Another said he would choose a copy of Milton's writings. Another thought he would want to have Browning's sonnets. Finally Chesterton's turn came. He was reported to have said that he would not want the Bible or Milton or Browning or Shakespeare inasmuch as he could recall enough passages from those books for his own inspiration. The *one* book he would most desire in such a situation would be a copy of *A Manual for Amateur Boat Builders!*

Of course! And I strongly suspect there are times and situations in which God Himself needs boat builders more than poets, compassionate traveling salesmen more than preoccupied priests along modern Jericho Roads, mothers more than nuns, men of integrity in the marketplace more than preachers in the pulpits, money and muscles and jobs and laws more than hymns and prayers. All of which suggests that no one of us has any reason to despise the importance of his own role or to underestimate the importance of the other fellow's.

But now we are ready to add one more statement to our formula for devoting our wills to God's purpose. God needs you as much as you need God. God needs "them" as much as He needs us. But the consideration that really puts the bite into this business of trying to do God's will is that God needs each of us *now* as much as He needs any of us ever.

Long before the hippie and psychedelic movement put its proper emphasis on living *now*, the advertising men had discovered the importance of the present tense. One of them advised:

> No tense suggests action as vividly as the present tense. Try never to let your copy promise that your product or service can, will, might, could, would or ought to do something for the reader. Make your prospect know that your product does what you claim for it. Make him feel that it is happening right while he reads. So—"Old Dutch Cleanser CHASES Dirt"—not—"Old Dutch Cleanser might conceivably remove the accumulated filth if properly applied."

Paul understood the importance of the present tense. He did not say, "God might conceivably work through you at some distant time in the nebulous future." Paul said, "God works through different persons in different ways." The realization of this fact and the consequent development of our capacity to live in the present tense becomes one of the surest marks of spiritual stature.

Albert Schweitzer was awarded the Nobel Peace Prize for 1952. An American correspondent happened to visit Schweitzer just at the time the announcement was made. He found Schweitzer busy as you might expect him to be. He was working on the expansion of his leper colony. He told the correspondent he was turning the $33,800 award money over for this expansion program. The correspondent asked Dr. Schweitzer to describe his reaction to the award. The famous man replied that he was greatly honored and pleased. "But," he added, "no man has the right to pretend that he has worked enough for the cause of peace or to declare himself permanently satisfied."

Then Schweitzer went on to tell the correspondent that he was not going to Oslo to receive the award because he was so busy working on the leper colony. As a matter of fact, according to the correspondent's wire, Dr. Schweitzer broke off the interview quite abruptly to tend to the broken leg of an African patient who had just arrived by dugout canoe. The capacity to get to work on the broken leg presently in front of you—rather than to revel in the Nobel Prize awarded for past achievement—that is spiritual maturity.

For all of us—NOW is always the time for serving God, as near as the closest need and as ready as a friendly smile. To every man, each new day opens another door of opportunity through which to move in the direction of devotion to God's Kingdom of Love.

Don Blanding said this poetically in a more vivid way than my prose. He wrote, "I was seated in front of the General Sherman tree, supposedly the oldest, largest living thing on earth, thirty-two and a half feet through and two hundred and sixty-seven and a half feet high, which gives no adequate idea of its vast self. A gnat came buzzing around my head, I gave it a puff of smoke and it withdrew to the great tree where it flitted and shimmered in a beam of light. It seemed to be talking to the great tree. I wondered what a gnat would have to say to a great tree, and this is what I heard:

The tiny gnat with a wee thin voice spoke to Sequoia tree
I am the least of living things, would you deign to speak to me?
You must be God . . . or the brother of God . . . so solid and great
  and tall.

Doing Our Thing

Sequoia spoke from its mighty height, "We are only large or small,
Not greater or less in the eyes of God. We are his children, all.
Once I was less than the size of you, a germ of growth in a seed,
Driven to reach for the passing cloud by a silent urgent need.
Now I am tall, as men count tall, yet you with your shining wings
Can mount to the sky above my head for a God's-eye view
   of things.
To the mountain's gaze I am just as small as you seem small to me.
In the heart of God we are all the same, mountain, gnat and tree.
A life is as long as each may live, eon, millennium, day.
Each is a thought in the Mighty Mind, each perfect in his way.
We can repay, each in his way (God won't ask more than that)
If I try to be the mightiest tree and you be the gnattiest gnat.*

How can you devote your will to God's purpose? You may be
helped to your own answer if you remember: God needs you as
much as you need God; God needs "them" as much as He needs
us; and God needs each of us now as much as He needs any of us
ever.

We can repay, each in his way (God won't ask more than that)
If I try to be the mightiest tree and you be the gnattiest gnat.

---

* Don Blanding, "Gnat and the Sequoia" in *Mostly California* (New York: Dodd,
Mead & Company, 1948), p. 21.